T0387477

Get Motoring!
Trucks

by Dalton Rains

www.focusreaders.com

Copyright © 2024 by Focus Readers®, Mendota Heights, MN 55120. All rights reserved. No part of this book may be reproduced or utilized in any form or by any means without written permission from the publisher.

Focus Readers is distributed by North Star Editions:
sales@northstareditions.com | 888-417-0195

Produced for Focus Readers by Red Line Editorial.

Photographs ©: Shutterstock Images, cover, 1, 4, 7 (top), 9 (top), 9 (bottom), 11 (top), 11 (bottom), 13, 15 (top), 15 (bottom), 16 (top left), 16 (top right), 16 (bottom left), 16 (bottom right); iStockphoto, 7 (bottom)

Library of Congress Cataloging-in-Publication Data
Names: Rains, Dalton, author.
Title: Trucks / by Dalton Rains.
Description: Mendota Heights, MN : Focus Readers, [2024] | Series: Get
    motoring! | Includes index. | Audience: Grades K-1
Identifiers: LCCN 2023033155 (print) | LCCN 2023033156 (ebook) | ISBN
    9798889980124 (hardcover) | ISBN 9798889980551 (paperback) | ISBN
    9798889981404 (pdf) | ISBN 9798889980988 (ebook)
Subjects: LCSH: Trucks--Juvenile literature.
Classification: LCC TL230.15 .R34 2024 (print) | LCC TL230.15 (ebook) |
    DDC 629.224--dc23/eng/20230731
LC record available at https://lccn.loc.gov/2023033155
LC ebook record available at https://lccn.loc.gov/2023033156

Printed in the United States of America
Mankato, MN
012024

About the Author

Dalton Rains is a writer and editor who lives in Minnesota.

Table of Contents

Trucks 5

Parts 6

Uses 12

Glossary 16

Index 16

Trucks

Trucks drive on **roads**.

They can move many things.

They bring goods to people and **stores**.

Parts

The front of the truck
is called the **tractor**.
The inside of the tractor
is called the cab.
Some cabs have beds inside.

The tractor pulls a **trailer**.

Some trailers carry boxes.

Some trailers carry logs.

trailer

Other trucks are made

in one piece.

The trailer does not come off.

A garbage truck carries trash.

A dump truck carries dirt

or rocks.

Uses

Some trucks are very large.

They can carry big loads.

They travel a long way.

Other trucks carry less.

They might travel across a city.

They might help people move to

a new house.

Glossary

roads

tractor

stores

trailer

Index

B
beds, 6

C
cabs, 6

D
dump trucks, 10

M
moving, 14